COLLECTABLES

Teddy
Bears

This is a STAR FIRE book

STAR FIRE BOOKS
Crabtree Hall, Crabtree Lane
Fulham, London SW6 6TY
United Kingdom

www.star-fire.co.uk

First published 2008

08 10 12 11 09

1 3 5 7 9 10 8 6 4 2

Star Fire is part of The Foundry Creative Media Company Limited

ISBN: 978 1 84786 195 5

Printed in China

Thanks to: Chelsea Edwards, Chris Herbert,
Gemma Walters and Nick Wells

Picture credits
Courtesy of Christie's Images Ltd: 21, 65. Courtesy of Christie's, London: 25, 37, 41, 43, 49, 51.
Courtesy of Foundry Arts: 31. Courtesy of Michael Pearson Photography. Bears courtesy of
Sue Pearson: 1, 3, 4, 7, 13, 15, 23, 29, 45, 47, 57, 59, 61, 63, 67, 69, 71, 72. Courtesy of Nick
Nicholson: 9, 11, 17, 19, 27, 35, 53, 55. Courtesy of Pat Rush: 39

Every effort has been made to contact all copyright holders. The publishers would be pleased
to hear if any oversights or omissions have occurred.

COLLECTABLES

Teddy
Bears

Posy Carpenter

STAR FIRE

FOREWORD

Teddy bears offer so much joy and comfort
that we have all become accustomed to their
inviting presence in our lives. They provide a
nostalgic, personal reassurance of an ideal
past, whilst bringing us strength for the battles
of our daily lives. The teddy bear itself has
a rich and glorious history which this little
book celebrates in its own special way.
A wonderful book to dip in and out of,
to enjoy and to keep by your side, we hope
that TEDDY BEARS will bring you years
of quiet pleasure.

An arctophile is the name
given to a person that collects
or is fond of teddy bears.

❈

HOW THE TEDDY BEAR
GOT HIS NAME

In November 1902, President Theodore 'Teddy' Roosevelt visited Mississippi to settle a border dispute between that state and Louisiana. While there, he went hunting, but refused to shoot a bear that had been captured for him. Such an act would have been far too unsportsmanlike.

The incident was immortalized by the
work of political cartoonist Clifford
Berryman. His cartoon, 'Drawing the
line in Mississippi', appeared on the
front page of the Washington Post
two days after the event.

DRAWING
THE LINE
IN MISSISSIPPI

Berryman 1902

CLIFFORD K. BERRYMAN'S EPOCH-MAKING CARTOON
NOVEMBER 10, 1902

The appealing little bear began to appear alongside the President in other Berryman cartoons, and in no time at all the whole country was captivated.

It was not until 1906, however, that the name Teddy Bear was used. Berryman referred to his creation as the Roosevelt Bear, and to Roosevelt himself, he was known as the Berryman Bear.

The record for the 'Smallest Commercially Available Stitched Teddy Bear' is held by Cheryl Moss. In 2003 she made a mini bear, measuring only 9 mm (0.29 in) in height!

1958 was the year that
Paddington made his first appearance
in the UK in Michael Bond's
A BEAR CALLED PADDINGTON.

The famous Steiff 'Button-in-ear' trademark was introduced and patented in 1905.

❈

Following the tragic sinking of the Titanic in 1912, Steiff produced 600 black bears and shipped them to London as a symbol of mourning.

❋

For every bear that ever there was
Will gather there for certain because
Today's the day the Teddy Bears have their picnic.

Jimmy Kennedy, 'The Teddy Bears Picnic'

'Teddy Girl' was the name of the most expensive bear ever sold at auction. She fetched a record-breaking £110,000 at Christie's.

The story behind 'Teddy Girl' undoubtedly added value to her, as she was owned by Colonel T.R. Henderson – founder of the British branch of the charity Good Bears of the World.

Winnie-the-Pooh first appeared
in the magazine PUNCH on
13 February 1924.

To begin with Winnie-the-Pooh
was known as Edward Bear.

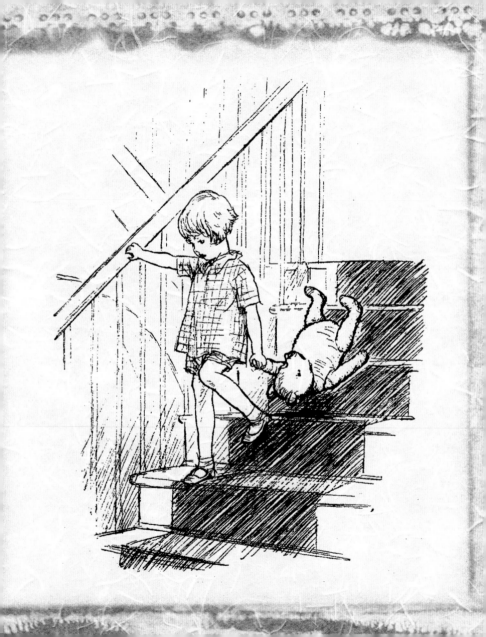

Bearabilia can range from crockery to figurines and from silverware to glassware.

※

Rupert the Bear was first
seen at the bottom of the woman's
page in the DAILY EXPRESS on
8 November 1920.

※

Rupert ... and The Old Miser

By Mary Tourtel

RUPERT OF THE
Daily Express

NOVELTY BEARS 1

Manufacturers created novelty bears in an attempt to beat the competition and produce a teddy that was original. Some of the novelty bears created were Steiff's musical clown from Harrods and Bing's Footballing Bear.

NOVELTY BEARS 2

Clockwork played a key role
in the production of early
novelty bears and they are all
now highly collectable.

NOVELTY BEARS 3

Other novelty bears include electric eye bears, which were made by several American companies. When the belly or ear of the bear was squeezed the bulbs in the eyes would light up.

✻

FAMOUS BEARS 1

Alfonzo was a bright red Steiff bear, bought by George Mikhailovich, Grand Duke of Russia, for his daughter Princess Xenia. The bear remained with the princess until her death and was auctioned at Christie's in 1989 fetching a massive £12,100.

FAMOUS BEARS 2

Elliot was identical to Alfonzo except that he was bright blue. He was sent to Harrods in 1908 with other coloured Steiff bears and fetched a staggering £49,500 at Christie's auction house in 1993.

✠

THE CHARACTERISTICS OF
AN EARLY STEIFF BEAR

- Humped back
- Long shaved muzzle
- Long arms with paws curving up
- Long legs, narrow ankles and
  large feet
- Button in left ear
- Good quality mohair

THE CHARACTERISTICS OF
AN EARLY IDEAL BEAR

- Triangular head with wide forehead, long muzzle and ears set wide apart
- Long, slender torso with humped back
- Long arms, curved at paws
- Pointed toes
- Short-pile mohair fur

THE CHARACTERISTICS OF
A TYPICAL **BING** BEAR

- Large head and ears
- Long muzzle, closely shaved
- Humped back
- Metal label with the
  letter BW in black fixed
  to right arm
- Large feet
- Long, shaggy mohair

*E*arly bears were filled with wood wool – long, thin wood shavings. Which was later replaced by softer kopak, but the 1950s saw a demand for washable materials and that is when foam chippings appeared. Now bears are mainly stuffed with polyester.

THE MOST POPULAR
TEDDY BEAR NAMES

Edward

Teddy

Ted

Eddie

Theo/Theodore

The music for 'The Teddy Bears Picnic' was composed in 1907 by John W. Bratton, but it wasn't until 1930 that lyrics were added by Jimmy Kennedy.

TEDDY QUOTES 1

'The Teddy has physical qualities
which make an immediate, unselfish appeal.
One knows instinctively that they are there to
help and woe betide the person, of whatever
age, suddenly deprived of their services.'

Peter Bull, BEAR WITH ME

TEDDY QUOTES 2

'If you're sick or lonely
in a hospital bed,
love IS a Teddy Bear.'

James T. Ownby, founder of
Good Bears of the World

FAMOUS
ARCTOPHILES 1

The best-known arctophile ever was British actor Peter Bull. His teddy bear 'Theodore' travelled in his pocket wherever he went.

✻

FAMOUS
ARCTOPHILES 2

Elvis's treasured 1909 Steiff bear, Mabel, was bought by English Aristocrat, Benjamin Slade. Mr Slade loaned Mabel to a museum where he was viciously mauled by the guard dog, Barney, who was meant to be keeping the display of valuable bears safe!

✺

According to the Royal Alberta Museum, 40% of adults still have their childhood teddy bear.

❋

A collection of teddy bears
is sometimes referred to as a
'hug' of bears.

TEDDY QUOTES 3

'*I* don't think my name is likely to be worth much in the toy bear business, but you are welcome to use it.'

Theodore (Teddy) Roosevelt, 1903

TEDDY QUOTES 4

'They are there when wanted but quite content to await your pleasure...an ideal recipe for the perfect friendship.'

Michael Bond

TEDDY QUOTES 5

'There's nothing childish about Teddy Bears! They are no more childish than collecting wives, cars or yachts.'

Peter Bull

❊

Come back soon!